Stray
Sock
Sewing

Making Unique,
Imaginative
Sock Dolls
Step-by-Step

By Daniel

NORTH LIGHT BOOKS

Cincinnati, Ohio
www.mycraftivity.com

Stray Sock Sewing
Copyright © 2006 Apple House Publishing, Taiwan.
English language rights, translation & production by
World Book Media LLC.
E-mail: info@worldbookmedia.com
For international rights inquires contact: info@worldbookmedia.com
First published in the United States of America in 2008 by North Light Books, an imprint of F+W
Publications, Inc.
4700 East Galbraith Road, Cincinnati, Ohio 45236. (800) 289-0963. First edition.

Distributed in Canada by Fraser Direct
100 Armstrong Avenue
Georgetown, ON, Canada L7G 5S4
Tel: (905) 877-4411

Distributed in the U.K. and Europe by David & Charles
Brunel House, Newton Abbot, Devon, TQ12 4PU, England
Tel: (+44) 1626 323200, Fax: (+44) 1626 323319
E-mail: postmaster@davidandcharles.co.uk

Distributed in Australia by Capricorn Link
P.O. Box 704, S. Windsor, NSW 2756 Australia
Tel: (02) 4577-3555

Library of Congress Cataloging-in-Publication Data

Daniel
Stray Sock Sewing: Making One of a Kind Creatures from Socks / Daniel.
p. cm.

ISBN-10: 1-60061-199-0
ISBN-13: 978-1-60061-199-5

12   11   10   09   08   5   4   3   2   1

Printed in China

fw

F+W PUBLICATIONS, INC.
www.fwpublications.com

explore your creativity making sock dolls

introduction

I began working in the advertising industry in the 1980s, and from then on, I spent twenty years being commercially creative, satisfying my clients' needs, and meeting deadline after deadline. I adapted to the crazy world of advertising, but I felt like a hamster on a wheel.

After a while, I began to question what was really right for me—professionally and creatively. I knew I needed to be truer to myself.

That's when I decided to leave advertising and find something that was a better fit for me. I realized that I like to be creative, but I needed to ditch the commercial rat race. During my transition out of advertising, I stumbled across sock dolls—these small creatures filled me with creative inspiration.

socks are not just socks

While browsing in a bookstore, I found a craft book from Japan that used mittens and socks to make dolls. I bought that book and when I got home, I tried my hand at doll-making with one of my stray socks. It took me more than three hours, with my clumsy, "manly" hands, but I finally made my first sock doll.

I quickly got really good at making these dolls and was amazed at how each doll turned out uniquely with such distinct and adorable characteristics. Soon, friends started to ask me to make sock dolls for them. Everyone just loved them. These weren't just dolls. They were more like little pets with unique personality traits.

teaching sock-doll sewing classes?

One day, I saw a note on my blog from a technology company that wanted to offer their employees some fun creative classes. They asked if I would teach a class on making sock dolls.

I began jotting down notes on making my sock dolls and soon started teaching. Over time, as I taught more classes, I got better and better at explaining the techniques, from beginner to advanced levels.

Once, in one of my classes, a student was upset because she failed to sew a sock into a cute rabbit.
I said, "There's no failure in sock-doll making, but let's rework it."
We eventually converted the rabbit into a fat baby duck and it was extremely cute! The adaptation was a good example of how things always seem to work out in sock-doll making.

It's me, the rabbit converted into a fat duck.

have fun and see what happens!

Every sock doll that you'll make will be unique and a little quirky. In this book that is exactly what you will find—all my sock dolls have different personalities and unique stories of their own. I hope that when you finish this book you'll want to start tinkering with your stray socks. Have fun and see what happens!

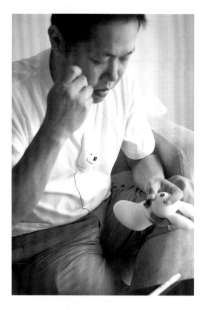

All About Sock Dolls

Contents

The Basics of Making Sock Dolls

PART 2

76
Materials and Tools

78
How to Choose Socks

81
1: Slip Stitch

82
2: Backstitch

83
3: Ladder Stitch

84
4: Straight Stitch to
Seal off Gaps

85
5: Split Running Stitch

86
6: Satin Stitch

88
7. How to Sew Buttons
and Beads

PART 3 Projects Step by Step

92
Long-Eared Mini Doll

96
Lucky Cat

102
Little Red Pig

108
Lace Rabbit

116
India Elephant

122
Teddy Bear

132
Punk Zebra

142
Bead-Eyed Hippo

PART 1

all about
sock dolls

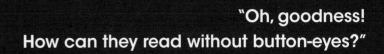
"Oh, goodness!
How can they read without button-eyes?"

Eating

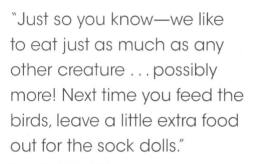

"Just so you know—we like to eat just as much as any other creature . . . possibly more! Next time you feed the birds, leave a little extra food out for the sock dolls."

Fitness

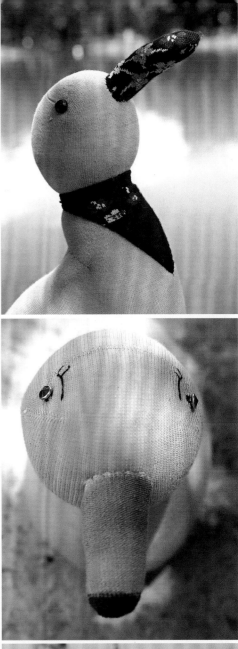

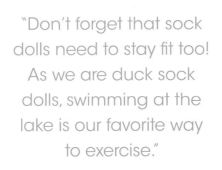

"Don't forget that sock dolls need to stay fit too! As we are duck sock dolls, swimming at the lake is our favorite way to exercise."

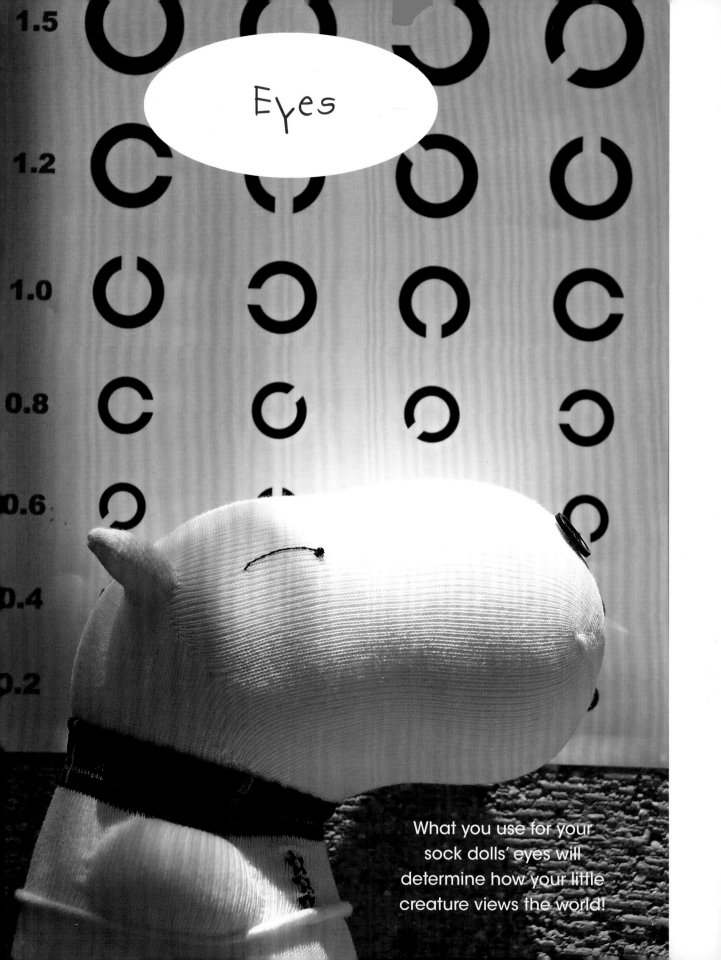

Eyes

What you use for your sock dolls' eyes will determine how your little creature views the world!

"People call me "bead eyes," but I don't care.
I like my little eyes. I see beauty in the little things."

Remember to schedule regular eye exams for your sock doll!

Love

"Everybody always thinks it's Cupid who's responsible for all of that love stuff. He points his arrow and boom—you fall in love."

"Well, forget about that. Really, it's my hoola-hoop and me hard at work. Next time you think you've been hit by Cupid's arrow, remember: the Love Cat has hooped you!"

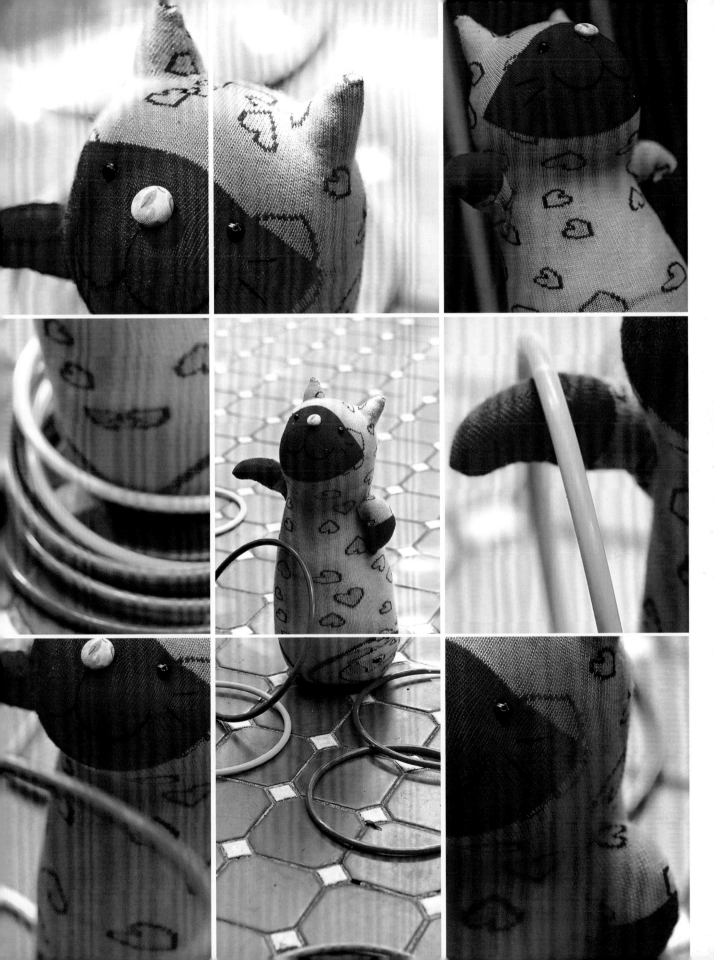

Happiness

"Om . . . Om . . ."

"We live in complicated times—sock dolls are here to make you happy!"

"May you be happy!

May you have peace!

May you take time to smell the potpourri in your sock drawer!"

Carpe Diem

"You might think that swimming is stupid if you are made of stuffing and old socks ... but life is about doing the impossible and the unexpected!"

"Seize the day and get your socks wet!"

"There's an impostor
in our midst!"

"Oh come on!
We're all sock dolls here!"

"So what if I look like a fish?"

27

"Goodness! We're acting like our stuffing's popped out! Now, let's mend our differences and have some darn fun!"

Haircuts

"Some people dread going to the dentist, but if you're a sock doll, hair cuts can be down right TEAR-ifying! Hey, you'd be nervous too if you were made of socks and stuffing!"

"Phew! Glad that's done!"

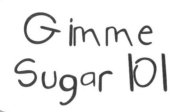

Sock dolls work hard to be so darn lovable!

Loyalty is the
stuffing sock dolls
are made of!

Loyalty

"We're always by your side."

"Woof!"

Play Time

Get out your action figures and have a little old-fashioned fun—Sock Doll vs. Transformers!

"Man, these guys are weak!
I'll let them take a few more
shots and then I'm gonna have
to show them who's boss . . . "

"OK! No more Mr. Nice Guy!"

"Fishy wanna play?

Why don't you want to play?

What's that? You think I'll have you for lunch?

Oh no! I'm a Sock-o-dile, not a Crocodile! We're nice!"

The SOCK-o-dile

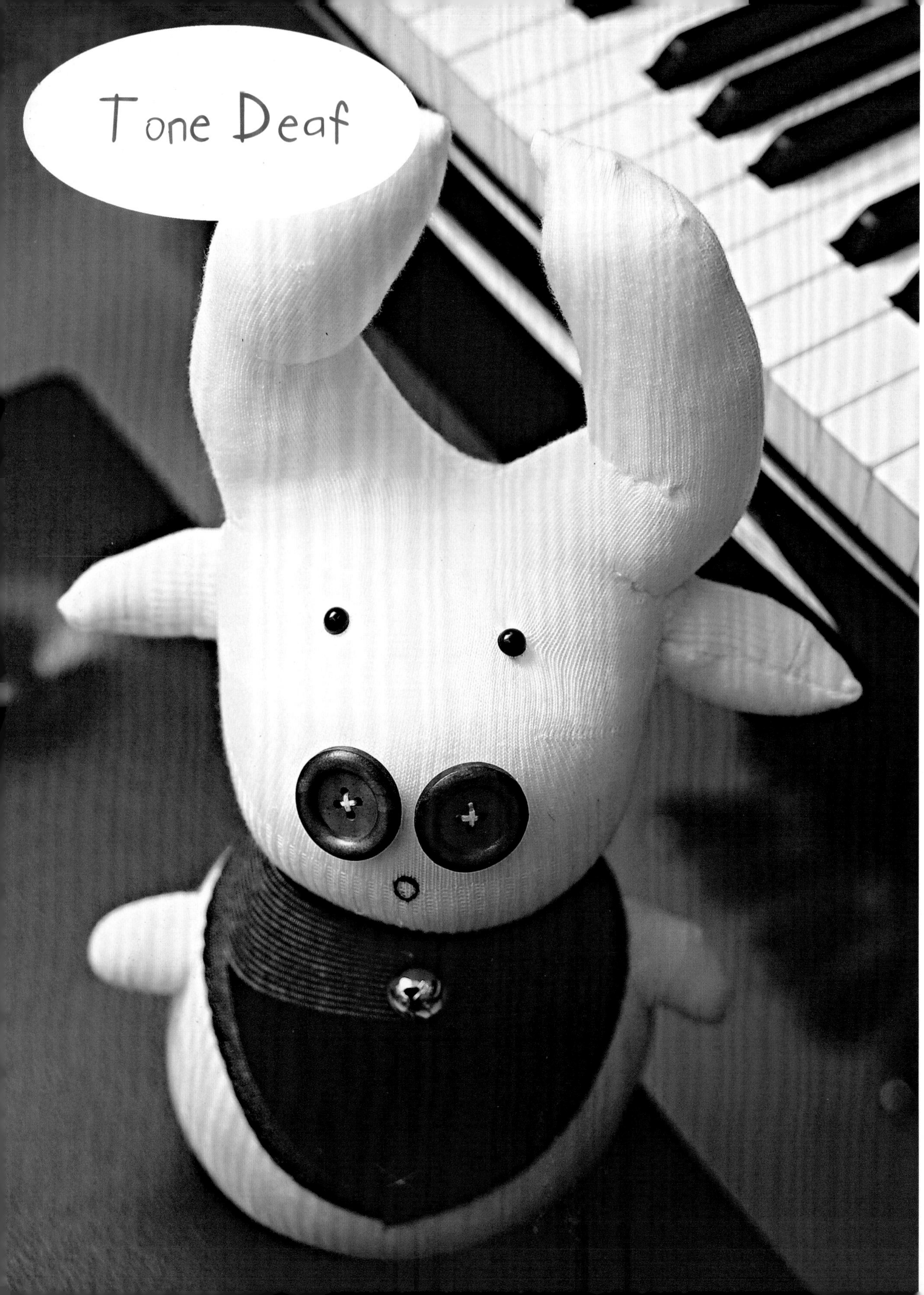
Tone Deaf

WARNING:
Buy earplugs if you encounter one of these sweet but musically challenged little creatures. They love to sing but are tragically tone deaf.

Hide & Seek Snapshots

"Here are some candid pictures of a few of us playing hide and seek."

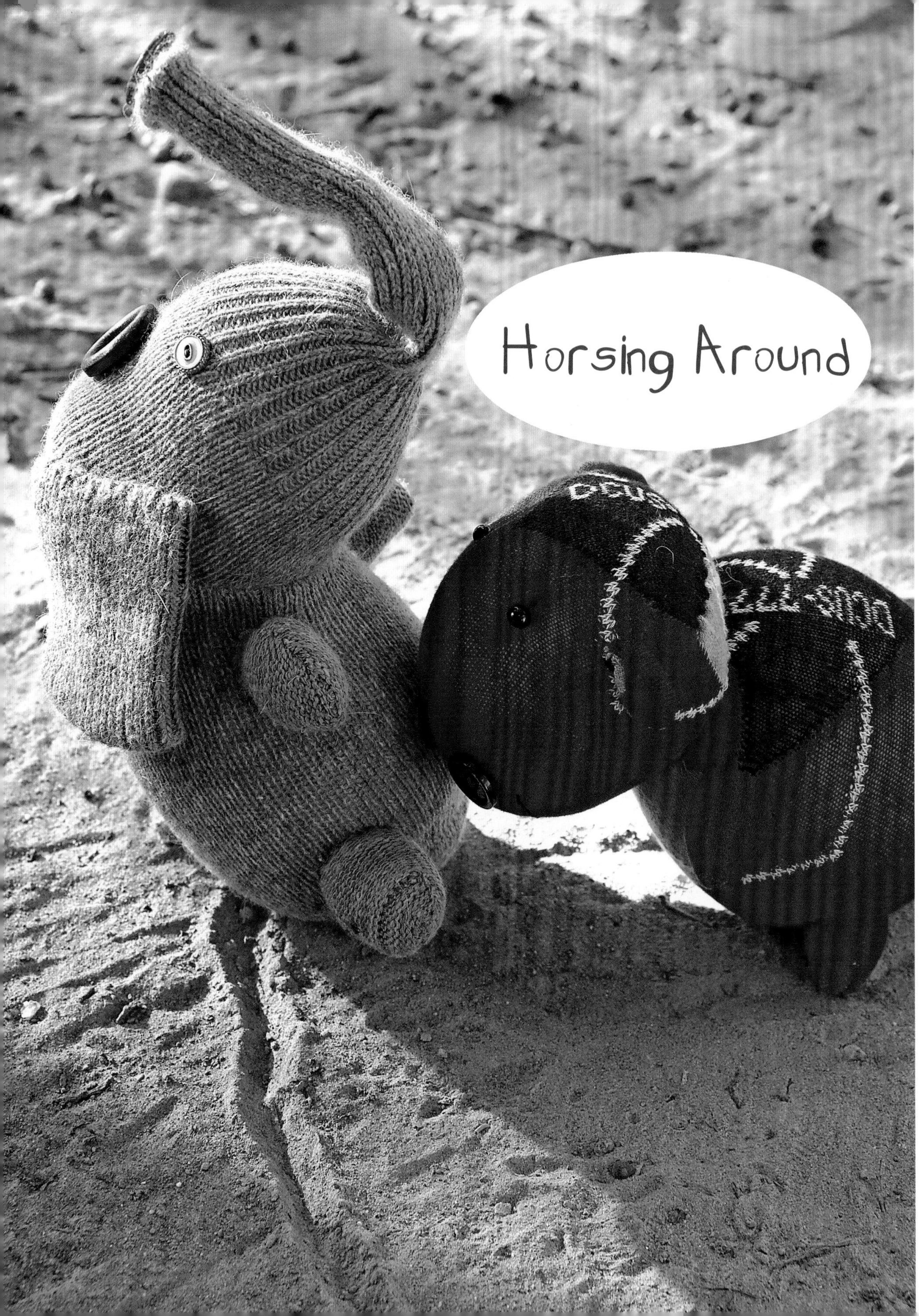
Horsing Around

These two guys aren't really fighting. Elephant and hippo sock dolls like to horse around a lot.

They can horse around all day—at least until it's time to eat!

Baby Sock
Dolls

A few words on these mini stuffed bundles of joy:

These little ones are pure joy, but they can't be left alone. Make sure to pack them in your bag before the start of your day—they are great travel companions! They're happy little dolls, ready to travel with you wherever you go.

"I fit in your pocket!"

Jealous Streak

I smell something funny.

Not all sock dolls get jealous—but the pigs,
especially the red ones . . . they do get jealous.

He's finally fallen asleep.
Now I can start snooping . . .
sniff, sniff, sniff . . .

"What's this smell? It's on his shirt, on his pants . . ."

"Oh no! He's found a new girlfriend! I've got competition!"

If you have one of these loving yet insanely jealous little red pigs and you start dating someone new, reassure your sock friend with extra hugs and attention. This will minimize any embarrassing acting out.

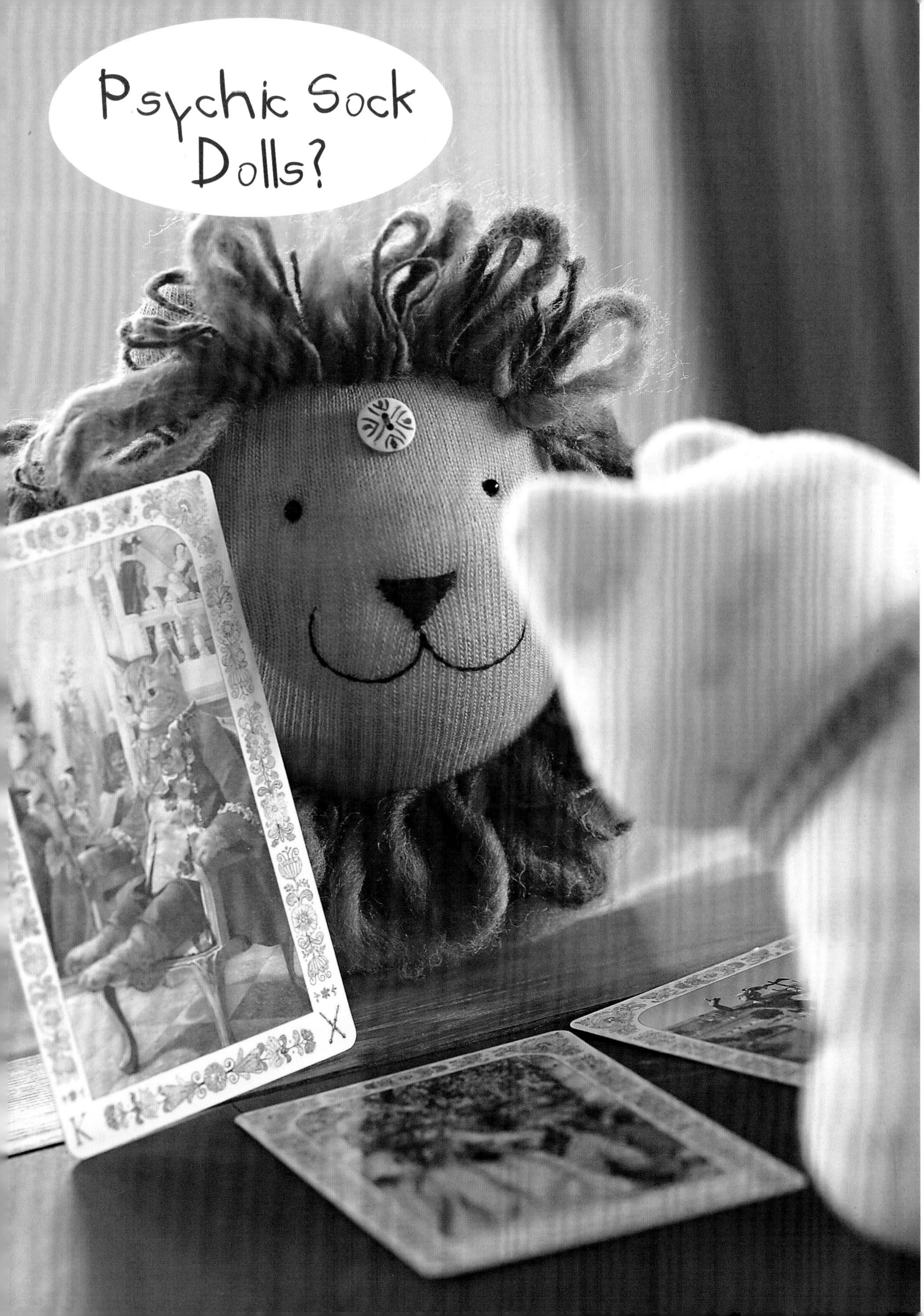
Psychic Sock Dolls?

Too bad the Lion King didn't know about the Tarot and crystal balls—he could have saved himself a lot of problems.

These little guys have an undisciplined streak.

Sock Doll
Tweens

For example, our little man here is standing
on his homework and refuses to move!

Getting them to go to
school, or do any task that
might be dull, requires
some "tough-love."

This will hurt you more
than it will hurt them . . .

Hawaiian Kona
(Bay View)

Puerto Rico
(yauco selecto)

Columbia Supremo
(San Augustin)

Brazil
sito soa joao

Coffee

Yemen
(mattari)

Panama boquete
(las victories)

Ethiopia Harrar
(horse)

Ethiopia
Yirgacheffe (Gr2)

Java
(top farms)

Tanzania peaberry
(kilimanjaro)

India Malabar
(monsoon)

Celebes kalossi
(Taraja)

By no means do all sock dolls like coffee. But this little one here lives for it! Meet the Coffee Addict. It is suspected that our little friend is stuffed with coffee beans. This theory has yet to be confirmed.

Make sure your cappuccino machine is in working order—you will be rewarded handsomely.

"Latte! Latte!"

Be careful! Sock doll BFF's are so innocent and sincere it could *hurt* if you look at them for too long!

Make a pair of these little love bears if you seek a double dose of adorable!

Rabbit
Reflections

"What would the world do without sock dolls?"

"I'm afraid of heights."

"Hey, you, down below, don't move around. Just look at the camera."

"I need to move for a side shot— it makes me look thinner."

"You guys are heavy! Let's get this shot over with!"

PART 2

the basics
of making
sock dolls

Lesson 1: Materials and Tools

A.

A. Needles

Pick different types of needles, depending on the size of your sock doll. Normally, I use longer needles to stitch the body, and shorter needles for details.

C. Scissors

Fabric scissors are great for cutting socks. You'll need a pair of sharp scissors that won't fray or snag the fabric. Small, pointed scissors are good for seam ripping.

B. Thread

I like to use upholstery thread for sewing big areas and closing the stuffing holes. Upholstery thread is very strong, and it can withstand a lot of pulling and tugging. Use thinner threads for eyes, mouths, and other detailed parts.

B.

C.

Daniel's Classroom Tips

When you pick thread, choose the types that have the most even thickness. Cheaper thread might not be woven uniformly.

Use quality needles because they can handle more tension and will not bend or break easily.

D. Writing Tools

Colored pencils or erasable marking pens are good for tracing patterns and marking fabric.

E. Stuffing

Cotton stuffing or polyester fiberfill can be used to stuff your sock dolls. You don't want to cram the doll—just stuff it with small pieces, bit by bit. You can use tweezers for filling smaller areas.

D.

E.

F.

F. Buttons and Beads

You can use buttons and beads for dolls' noses, eyes, and decorations. If you have a variety of buttons and beads to choose from, you'll have more options for creating original and unique characters.

Daniel's Classroom Tips

I encourage my students to keep all the buttons from their old clothes. Unique buttons can be expensive, and there is nothing better than recycling buttons from what you already have.

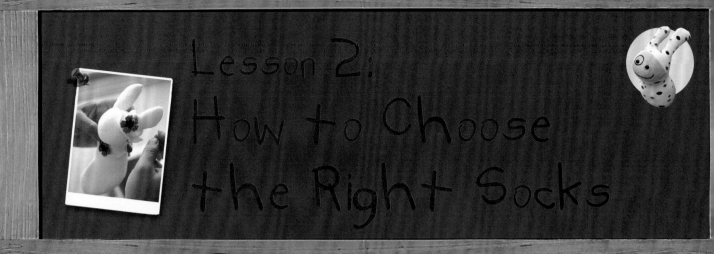

Lesson 2: How to Choose the Right Socks

A.

A. Socks with Patterns and Color

It's great for beginners to use socks with color blocks around the toe and heel areas. These color blocks highlight the shape of your sock doll and can become the base of your doll's color scheme.

B. Wool Socks

Wool socks will give your doll a thick, warm texture, and they're great for making sturdy creatures. However, it can be hard to sew details due to the loose weave.

C. Baby Socks

Baby socks are great for making smaller dolls. A cotton sock with soft stuffing will make a cuddly mini doll. Use stretchy baby socks to make bigger sock dolls. You can also use regular socks to make baby dolls.

B.

C.

Daniel's Classroom Tips

Cotton and nylon socks can be very stretchy. When you pick these types of socks, try to stretch them a little bit to check how sheer they can be. You don't want to stuff stretchy socks too full, as they can become thin, and then you can see through to the white stuffing. Very thin socks might even break.

D. Knee Socks

Knee socks are good for making larger dolls or super-long shaped dolls.

E. Socks with Frilly Cuffs

There are lots of girl's socks with pretty cuffs made from lace, cotton, or wool. I often use these socks to make "Victorian Style," frilly dolls.

D.

E.

G.

F.

F. Inside-out Socks

You will often find there are totally different patterns and textures on the insides of your socks. Use your imagination, and take advantage of those unusual inside-out sock variations to make some unique dolls.

G. Scrap Fabric

Don't throw away the cut off parts from your socks or leftover fabric. You can use these leftovers as decorations or part of your next doll.

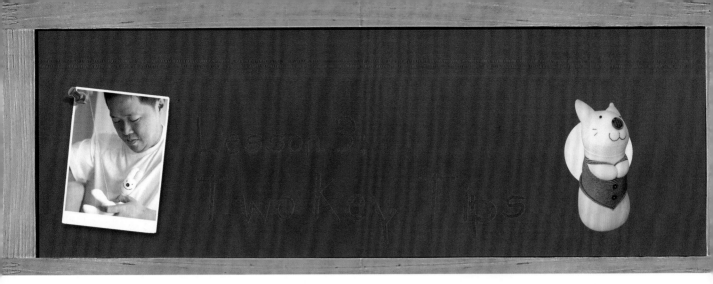

A. Estimating Thread Length

I prefer the length of my thread to be about the length of my arm. If the thread is too long, it could get tangled or knotted easily. If the thread is too short, you'll waste too much time on rethreading the needle, and you'll be left with too many knots.

B. Making a French Knot

1 Use your left hand to hold the needle and the thread. Tightly loop the thread around the needle two to three times with your right hand.

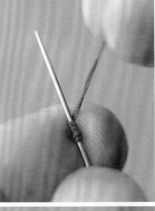

2 Compress the loops together, then hold the loops with your left hand.

3 Pull the needle out from the top, while holding onto the loops.

4 Tighten the knot.

Here are seven stitches that will help you make the projects in this book.

Number 1: Slip Stitch

This is an excellent hemming and finishing stitch because the thread is hidden inside a fold when it's sewn properly. The needle "tunnels" between the layers of the folded edges—hence the word "slip."

1 First, start the needle from behind the fold on the hem allowance, to hide the knot.

2 Take up around ⅛ inch (0.3 cm) of fabric; pull the thread.

3 Then about ¹⁄₁₆ inch (1 mm) below the fold and slightly behind it, tunnel the needle for about ¼ inch (0.6 cm), before you bring it through for the next stitch.

4 Pull the thread, finish the one-stitch cycle, and repeat. You will see the thread is mostly hidden inside the material.

Number 2: Backstitch

Backstitch is great for outlining the shape of your dolls' hands, feet, and ears. Turn the fabric inside out; this will hide the stitches when you turn it right side out again to stuff.

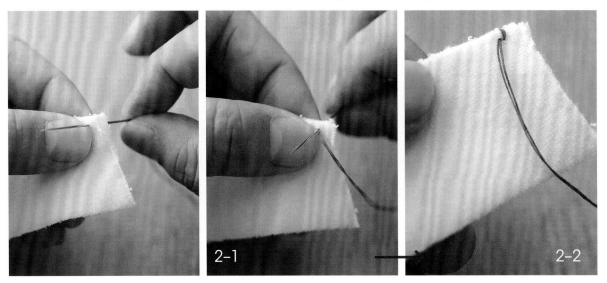

2-1

2-2

1 Right at the edge, bring the thread up from behind.

2 Loop the edge and go through the thread one more time, to make a knot. You'll want to make the stitches tight because once the doll is stuffed, the gaps can be expanded to expose the stuffing if you do not stitch tightly.

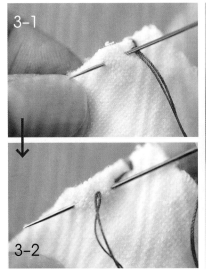

3-1

3-2

3 Run the needle through the material, around ⅛ inch (0.3 cm) in length. Re-enter the needle at the spot before where the previous stitch comes out. You've basically stitched back.

4 Use your thumb and index finger to hold the material flat, then pull the thread. To prevent the material from puckering together, do not pull the thread too taut.

5 This is how a completed backstitch should look.

Number 3: Ladder Stitch

Ladder stitching is a good way to attach dolls' parts together, and it's easy for beginners to do. You will want to make the stitches as small as possible to prevent the stuffing from leaking out.

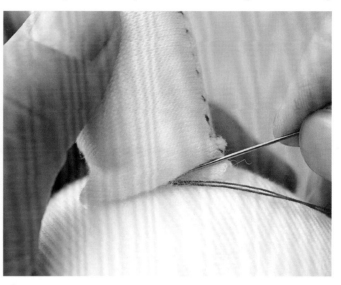

1 Place the parts in the right position, then sew from the main body part to the limb.

2 Before you push the thread through, use the side of the needle to push the edges back while you stitch. You'll want to push the edge back while you make each stitch. This way, you can hide the stitches mostly inside the seam.

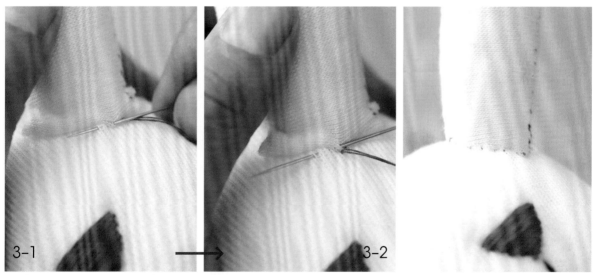

3-1

3-2

3 Stitch up and down through the two parts. Pin or hold the limbs together very steadily to avoid slipping.

4 This is how a finished section of ladder stitching should look.

Number 4: Straight Stitch to Seal off Gaps

The straight stitch is one of the easiest methods for sewing on large areas. You can use this stitch mainly to close the doll after you finished stuffing the body.

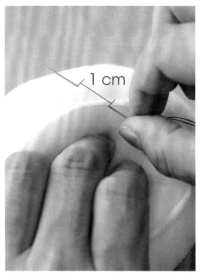

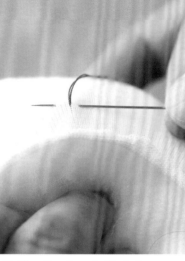

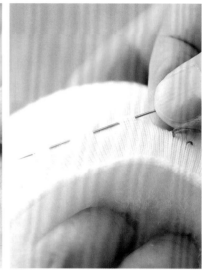

1 Bring the needle from inside to outside. Make the stitch no shorter than ⅜ inch (1 cm). If the stitch is too short, it could become loose easily.

2 Use the backstitch to sew at the same location again to make sure the hold of the initial stitches is steady.

3 Use the straight stitch to go around in a circle. While you are sewing, push the stuffing inside.

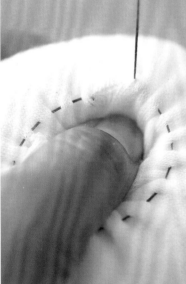

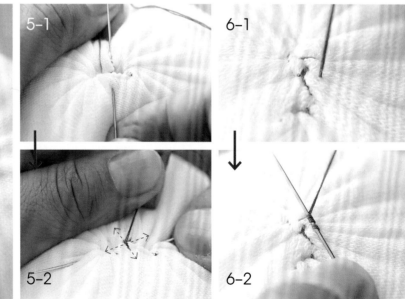

4 Pull the thread taut with each stitch, while pressing the stuffing inside.

5 When you stitch the opening shut, you can make the final stitches in the shape of a cross. The cross stitches will make the close-off even tighter.

6 Get the needle out from the middle of the hole and make a French knot.

Number 5: Split Running Stitch

The split running stitch can be used to outline a doll's mouth and eyes. You'll want to sew densely so that each stitch is blended together.

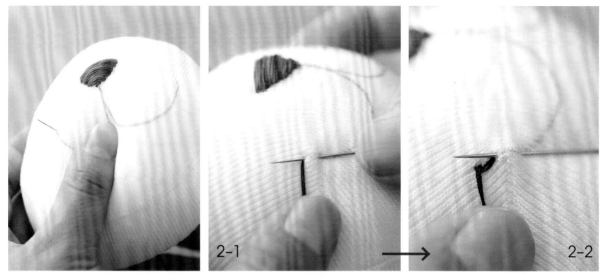

1 Use a colored pencil OR an erasable marking pen to trace the pattern first. Start the stitch from the inside, where you can hide the knot. Sew from the inside to outside.

2 Bring the needle ⅛ inch (0.3 cm) apart from the last stitch, then bring the needle from the front and back toward the last stitch. As the split stitch name implies, each new stitch is made through the previous one.

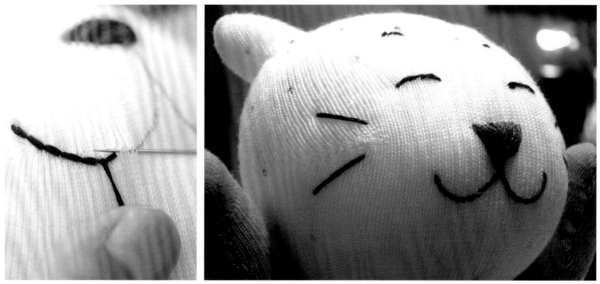

3 Trace the pattern with repeated stitches. Keep your stitch lengths as uniform as possible. When stitching a ∪ shape, pull the thread below the arc, then slip the needle between the threads for the next stitch.

4 When you've finished the first arc, you can turn the doll in a direction that is easy to work with for the next arc. I cross the needle to the other end of the arc, and stitch from the end toward the center.

5 Repeat the method used in step 2. If there is a ⌒ shape, pull the thread above the arc to sew through.

correct

incorrect

the crossed stitch

6 Note: If the arc is ⌒ shape, put the thread above the arc to stitch. If you leave the thread below the arc, the stitches will cross each other and look messy.

Number 6: Satin Stitch

Satin stitch is the universal filler. It is used here to fill a nose area.

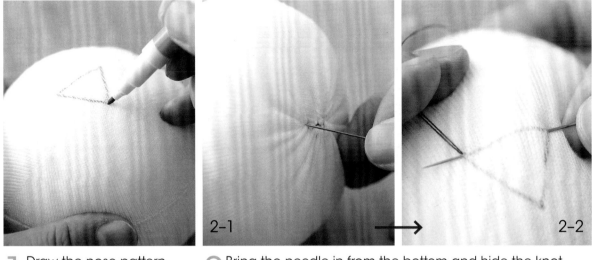

1 Draw the nose pattern.

2 Bring the needle in from the bottom and hide the knot inside. The needle should come out in the corner of the nose pattern.

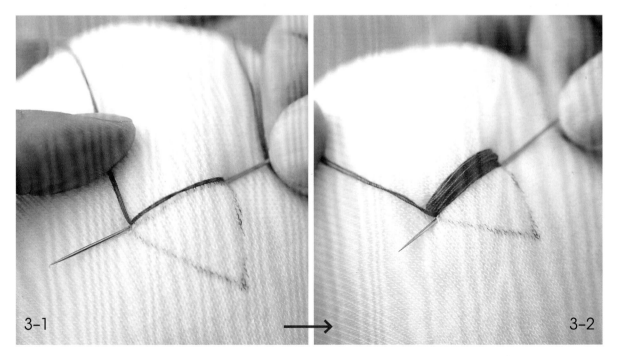

3 Continue to make stitches, laying them very close together but not over-lapping. To give the nose fullness, let the needle go through an ample amount of stuffing underneath. Since socks are very elastic and can stretch out of shape easily, you want your needle to catch as much stuffing as possible with each stitch. Otherwise, the pattern you filled could shrink or change shape.

4 When you sew to the end of the pattern, make a knot to fill the leftover gap.

5 After the knot, bring the needle back into the pattern, then cut the thread. This way, you will be able to hide the knot.

Number 7: How to Sew Buttons and Beads

Buttons or beads are mostly used for the eyes and noses of the sock dolls. You can also use them as decorative pieces for the body.

A: Using Cross Stitch for Buttons

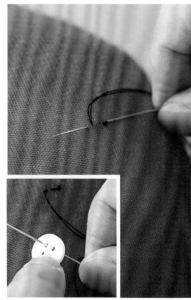

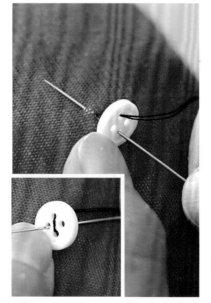

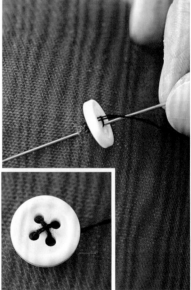

1 Use straight stitch to start. Pull the needle through one of the button holes.

2 Make stitches diagonally across the two holes, then repeat to stitch the other two holes across each other.

3 The stitches should appear like a cross.

B. Sewing a Button Shank

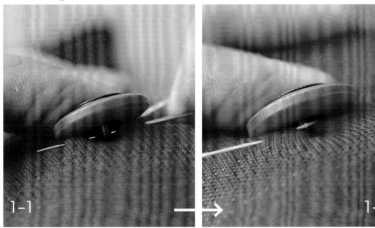

1 Using straight stitch, sew through the shank of the button. Repeat the stitch a few times, and make sure the shank is held down closely against the material. Make a knot to finish.

C. Sewing Beads

  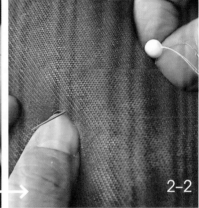

1 Sew the first bead at the desired location using straight stitch.

2 Bring the needle underneath the material, out at the location of the next bead.

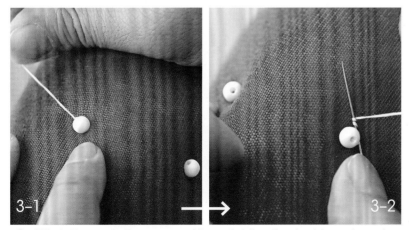

3 Stitch through the second bead. After the last bead, make a French knot to finish.

PART 3

projects step by step

1...2...3
Just follow me!

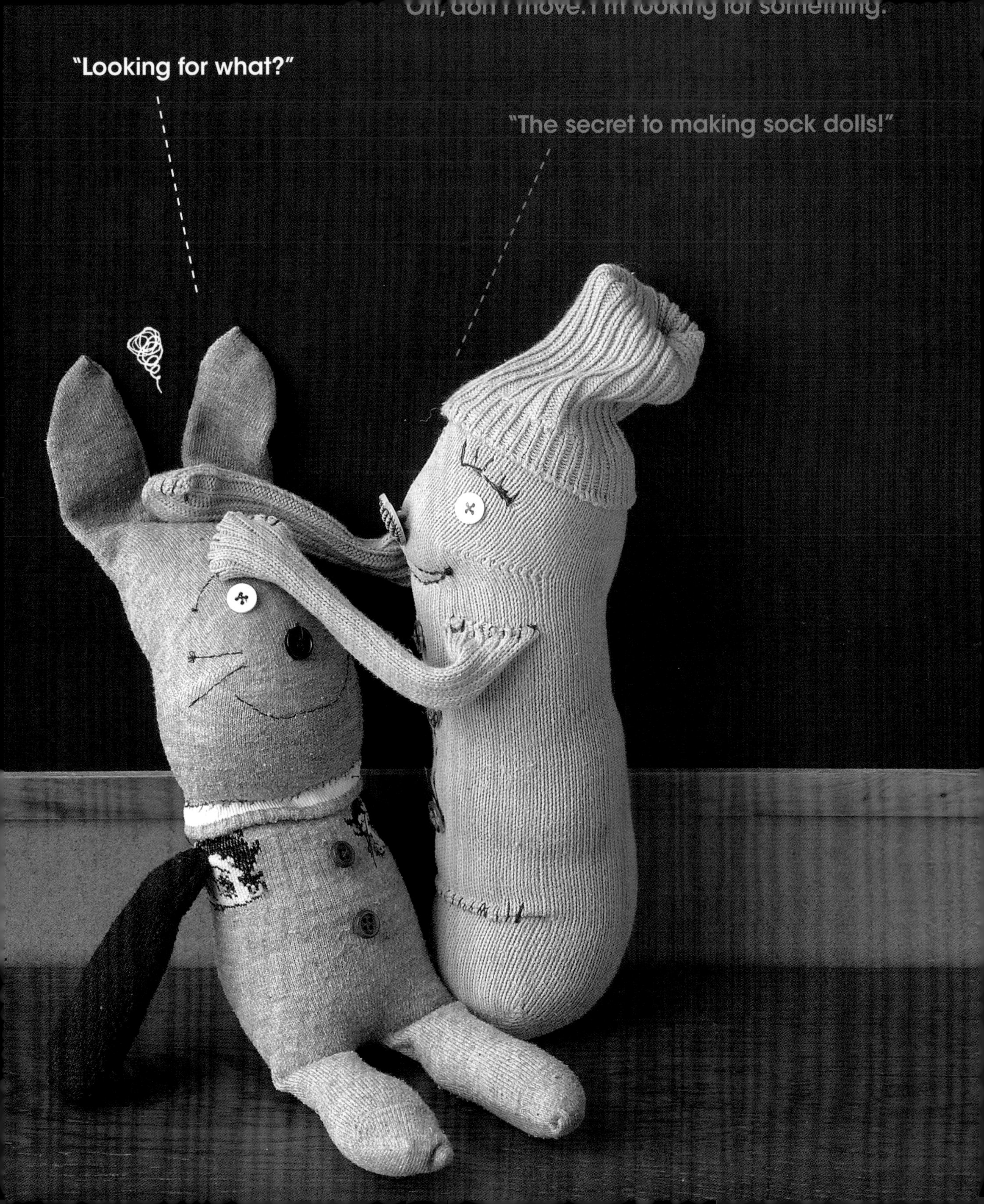
"Looking for what?"
"The secret to making sock dolls!"

Long-Eared Mini Doll

STEP BY STEP

Here's how to make a long-eared mini doll. (Although I'm not sure what to call this creature!)

Key Tips

1 If you can find a sock with slip-proof dots on the instep, you can use these dots as the beard.

2 Avoid overstuffing the sock to maintain the shape.

Materials and Tools

1 Threads in a variety of different thicknesses.

2 Needles, scissors, and marking pen.

3 Children's socks: Try to find socks that have a color block at the heel. This will become the face of the doll.

4 Stuffing.

  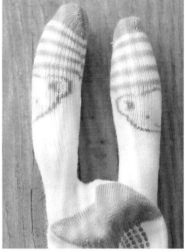

1 *Cut the tube part of the sock.*

Cut a U shape from the center of the tube, around ⅓ of the total sock length. Also cut a little hole on the toe, stuffing the doll.

2 *Use the backstitch to sew the shape of the ears.*

Turn the sock inside out and sew the ear shapes.

3 *Take two equal amounts of stuffing, and stuff them into the ears.*

Fill enough so that the ears can stand up.

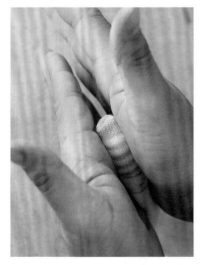 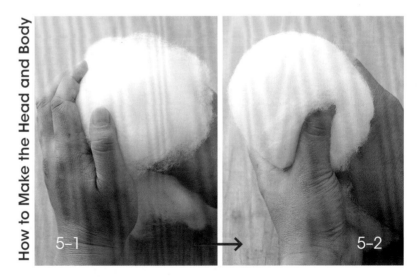

5-1 → 5-2

4 *Mold ears into the proper shape by rubbing gently.*

5 *Form the stuffing into a ball shape.*

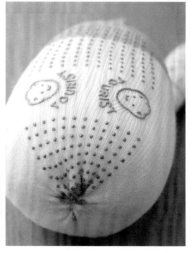

6 *Stuff the whole ball into the body.*

If there is too much or not enough stuffing, you'll need to pull it out. Remold the new amount into a ball shape, and fill it again. Don't try to patch in extra stuffing as the body will look uneven.

7 *Push the stuffing all the way up to the heel.*

Fill the heel with plenty of stuffing to create a very round shape. This will give the doll a lovely round face.

8 *Use the straight stitch to close off the hole at the bottom of the sock.*

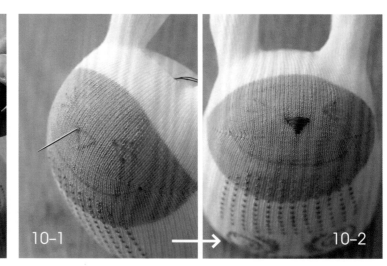

9 *Draw the face within the color-block area on the heel.*

10 *Use the satin stitch with thicker thread to fill in the nose area.*

10-1

10-2

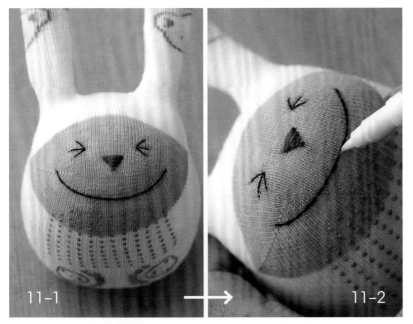

11-1

11-2

11 *Trace the pattern of the eyes and mouth.*

Using the split running stitch, sew along the traced outline with thick thread. If the pattern marks still show under the stitches, just erase them when you're done sewing.

12 *To make the doll stand up, gently press and mold the stuffing.*

You might need to press the bottom into a flat platform.

Daniel's Classroom Tips

There will be gaps in the stuffing that make the ears look uneven. Rub the ears after you fill with the stuffing, to make sure the stuffing is distributed evenly.
Left: Before rubbing, the ear shape is uneven.
Right: After rubbing, the shape becomes smooth and even.

Lucky Cat

STEP BY STEP

You might see this cat sitting at the doors of many Asian shops. The cat's right hand often swings back and forth. The swinging hand waves more customers into the store, and swings in more money. And that's why it's called the lucky cat.

Key Tips

1 Bend the top of the cat's hands downward to make it appear that he's waving.

2 Avoid overstuffing and mold them to look like waving hands. The cat's paws shouldn't look like a boxer with boxing gloves on.

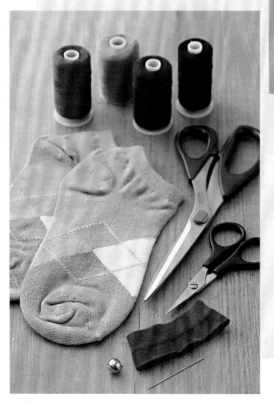

Materials and Tools

1 Thread, scissors, needles, and marking pen.

2 A pair of socks.

3 A bell.

4 A leftover cuff from another sock, to be used as the Lucky Cat's necklace.

5 Stuffing.

1 *Mold the stuffing for the body.*

You will need plenty of stuffing to make the cat an oval shape. Try to make the surface as smooth as possible.

2 *Stuff the sock.*

Insert the stuffing into one sock, only up to the heel. If there is not enough stuffing to fill the whole body, pull all the stuffing out and add extra stuffing. Remold and stuff again. You need to add the stuffing all at once to make the body look smooth.

3 *Finish off the body.*

Once the sock is filled in, press the neck part to form a pear shape.

4 *Mold the filling for the cat's head.*

Use a smaller amount of stuffing for the head, around ¼ of the amount of stuffing used for the body. Make sure you're extra careful to mold it into a nice, round ball shape. You want the cat to have a cuddly, smooth, round head.

5 *Stuff the head.*

Stuff the head so that it sits nicely on top of the body. Leave an opening at the back of the cat's head.

6 *Sew the opening.*

Use slip stitches to sew the seam together. At each end, there will be a corner left after sewing. Pull the corners upright, creating ears.

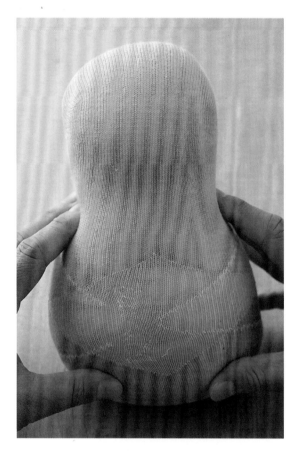

7 *Sculpt the cat.*

Gently mold the body shape. Make a thinner neck part, and smooth the stuffing out evenly.

"We're almost there!"

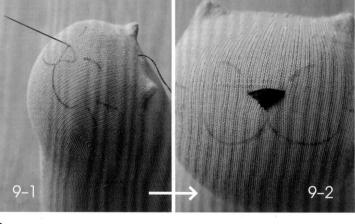

9-1   →   9-2

How to Make the Face

8 *Draw the face.*

Draw the face in proportion with the head area. The smiley face is the key to making this cat seem alive.

9 *Stitch the nose.*

Use the satin stitch to fill in the nose area. Start the needle from the seam at the back, and bring it out at one corner of the nose. Use thicker thread to give the nose area

10 *Stitch the eyes and the expression.*

Use thinner thread to outline the cat's eyes and expression. See detailed instructions on page 85.

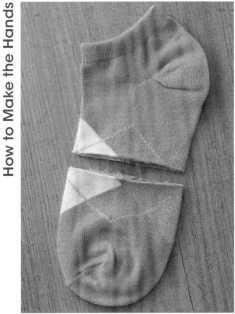

11 *Cut the other sock horizontally down the middle.*

We will use the toe and instep part of the sock to make two hands for the cat.

12-1 ➝ 12-2

12 *Fold the bottom half of the sock vertically down the middle.*

Make sure you fold the sock exactly in the middle, so the two hands are equal in size.

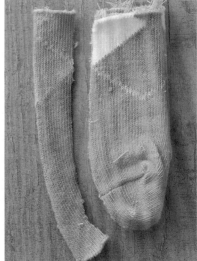

13 *Cut off around ⅜ inch (1 cm) along the fold.*

Cut the toe part of the sock into a round shape. This will make the arms slimmer.

14 *Turn the sock inside out. Use a dense running stitch to close off the seams.*

15 *Stuff the hands.*

Fill the hands with equal amounts of stuffing. Roll the hands back and forth to give them a smooth look. (See detailed instructions on page 95.)

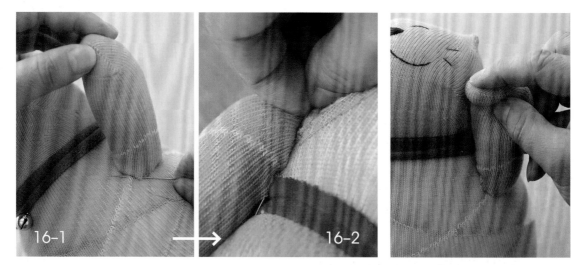

16-1　16-2

16 *Sew the hands to the body.*

Position the two hands just below the neck at the same level. Use the ladder stitch to sew the hands onto the body. To make sure they stand up, stitch the upper part of the hands to the body, as shown in Image 16-2.

17 *Press the hands.*

Press the top of one hand down, as if the hand is bending and waving.

Lesson One: Re-use Leftovers

If the cat falls easily because it has a heavier upper body, you can cut some of the leftover sock and roll it into a circle. Try to sit the cat into the circle cushion to give it a sturdier, flatter bottom (A–C).

Lesson Two: Decorating Your Cat

You can also use the leftover sock cuff to make a collar for the Lucky Cat. A nice little bell will be great on the collar, too. You can pick different-colored cuffs and necklaces, of course. Put the collar on the cat before attaching the hands.

Little Red Pig

STEP BY STEP

Key Tips

1 You'll need to use every part of one sock to make this pig. Proportion is the key here.

2 The hardest part of this project is possibly the ears. Often, the ears end up either too big or too small. You might need some practice before you can master the proper size of the ears.

Materials and Tools

1 Threads, needles, scissors, marking pen, and tweezers.

2 One single-colored sock and one sock with a curly cuff. Mix-and-match the colors of the socks for a colorful pig. The size of the socks will determine the size of the pig. I picked one white and one red sock with yellow trim.

3 Two black beads to use as the pig's eyes.

4 Two black buttons with four holes in the middle as the nostrils.

5 Stuffing.

6 Other decorations as you like.

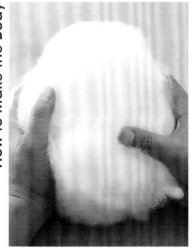

1 *Decide on the size of the stuffing.*

Mold the stuffing into a ball. The size of the sock and the amount of the stuffing will determine the size of your pig. For beginners, I recommend using socks for teens and molding the stuffing to fit into the palm of your hand.

2 *Fill the white sock.*

Remember to fill it in all at once. If you want to use less or more stuffing, pull the stuffing out and re-mold.

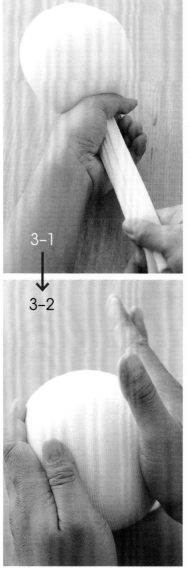

3–1

↓

3–2

3 *Push the stuffing all the way to the sock's toe.*

Pull the extra sock tight to condense the stuffing. Mold the stuffing into a ball.

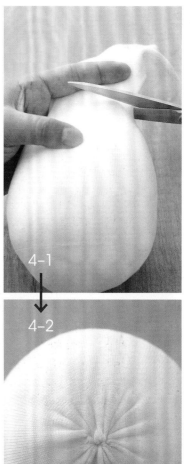

4–1

↓

4–2

4 *Cut off the extra sock.*

Stitch the hole shut as instructed on page 84.

5 *Partially cover the white ball with the red sock.*

Leave part of the white sock exposed, surrounded by the cuff of the colored sock. The white part that remains showing will become the pig's nose.

6 *Cut off any extra sock not used when you filled the ball.*

Make sure to cut in a straight line, right in the middle of the ball shape. Use the slip stitch to close the seam. Pull the red sock tight to ensure the seam will be right in the middle of the ball, opposite to the nose. The seam line will become the reference for the eyes and nose position on the face.

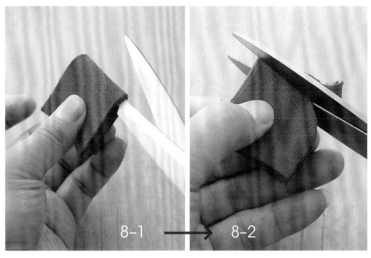

7   *Cut off a section of the leftover sock's instep to use as ears.*

8   *Fold in the middle and cut into two parts. Trim the edges into round corners.*

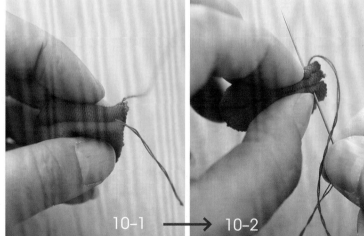

9   *Turn the sock inside out; use the backstitch to sew the round edges together.*

10   *Fold each ear in the middle. Stitch the bottom together to hold the folded ear shape.*

11 *Mark the location of the ears.*

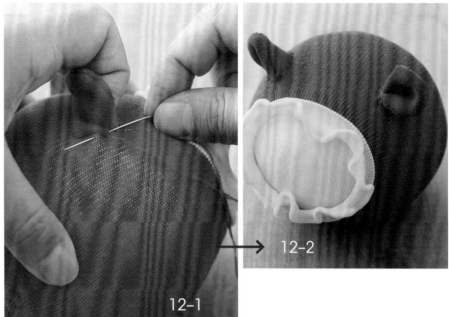

12-2

12-1

12 *Stitch the ears onto the body.*

13 *Mark the location of the eyes.*

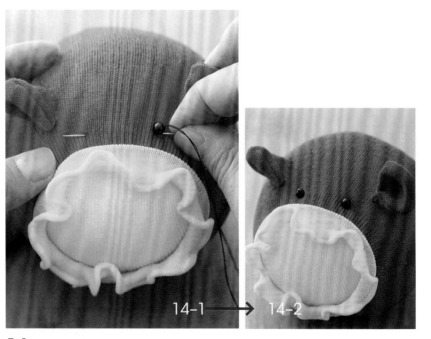

14-1 → 14-2

14 *Sew the beads on as the eyes. First bring the needle underneath the cuff to hide the knot.*

15 Take four equal amounts of stuffing, and mold them into four little balls.

16 Insert the balls between the white and red socks on the underside of the body. Squeeze the little balls so they pop out and show the shape of the feet.

17 Use the backstitch to sew around the four balls. Make sure to stitch through the white sock inside. Use close stitches to make a tight circle around the balls.

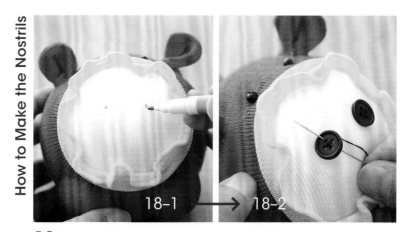

18 In a straight line down from the eyes, mark the position of the nostrils. Use cross stitch to sew on the two black buttons as the pig's nostrils. You've successfully made a sock pig!

Lace Rabbit

STEP BY STEP

Key Tips

1 This rabbit will have a lot of character if you give it a unique facial expression. Take extra care when sewing the smiley face, and also when judging the distance between the eyes.

2 Practice drawing the rabbit's face on some paper first. When you have learned to draw the right expression for the rabbit on paper, you can transfer it onto the sock.

Materials and Tools

1 Thread (black and white), in different thicknesses.

2 Needles, scissors, and marking pen.

3 Lace baby socks: two white, one pink.

4 Black beads for the eyes.

5 Flower-shaped button to use as the nose.

6 Stuffing.

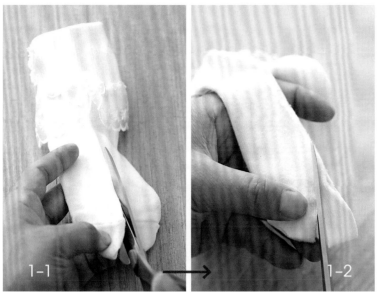

1 *Cut one white sock in the middle where the third toe would be. Cut down 3 inches (8 cm) into the sock. Trim the ends into points.*

3 *Use the other white sock, and repeat Step 1.*

The two separate parts of this sock will become the rabbit's ears. Cut off the cuff with the lace; the remaining in-step will be the head.

2 *Use the two cut tubes as the rabbit's legs. The instep above the legs will become the rabbit's body.*

109

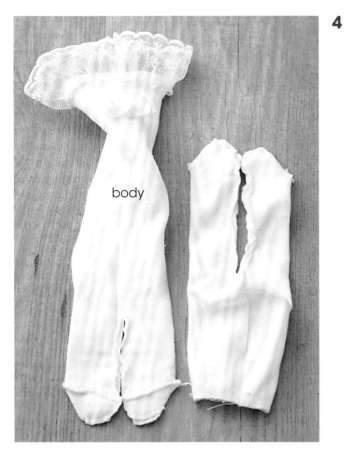

4 *Turn both socks inside out, and stitch the edges shut using the backstitch.*

body

6-1

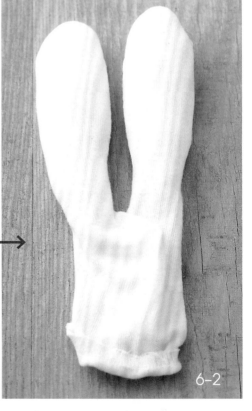

6-2

5 *Take equal amounts of stuffing to fill the ears.*

6 *Push the stuffing into each ear all at once. You don't want to fill the ears too full. Loosely stuffed ears will allow them to swing freely above the head.*

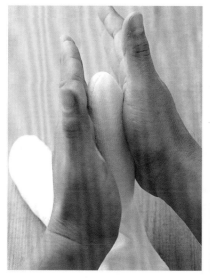

7 *Knead each ear with both hands gently, to make it into a uniform shape.*

8 *Mold the stuffing for the face.*

Take a large amount of stuffing. and mold it into a ball. Make the surface as smooth as possible to give the rabbit a nice, round face.

9 *Push the ball into the head part of the sock, all at once.*

If there is too much or not enough stuffing, pull it out, adjust the amount, and re-mold and return to Step 8.

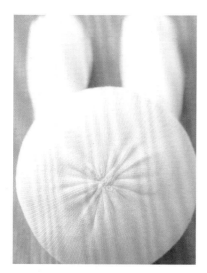

How to Make the Face

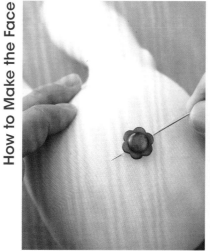

10 *Use straight stitching to stitch the opening of the head shut.*

11 *Sew on the button as the rabbit's nose.*

The nose is the focal point of the face, and it needs to be positioned first.

12 *Draw the rabbit's eyes, mouth, and whiskers.*

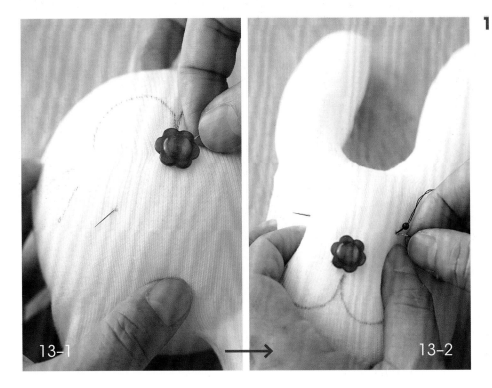

13-1

13-2

13 *To sew a bead as the eye, start the needle beneath the nose and bring it out at the point where the eye should be. This way, you can hide the knot.*

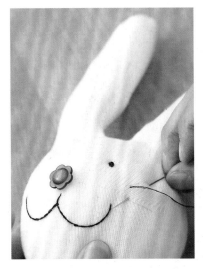

15-1

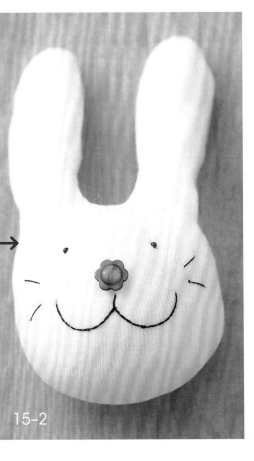

15-2

14 *Use the split stitch to outline the mouth and the whiskers.*

I suggest sewing the two sides of the whiskers and mouth separately, to avoid re-sewing the whole face if you make a mistake along the way.

15 *Once you stitch the face, erase any marking lines. Now you will have a lovely, smiley rabbit.*

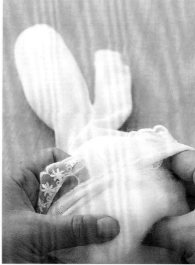

16 *Take two equal amounts of stuffing for the legs.*

You'll need more stuffing for the legs than for the ears, so that the legs will appear larger.

17 *Stuff both legs.*

Make sure both legs are stuffed fairly full to give them a sturdy look. Knead the legs with both hands to smooth them out.

18 *Stuff the body.*

Take a large amount of stuffing and mold it into an oval shape.

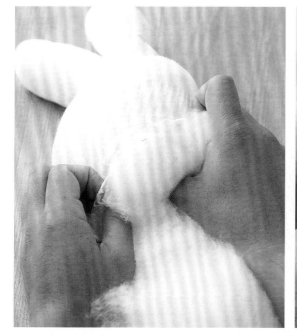

19 *Fill the body part of the sock. You want to stuff the body part full to give it a steady posture.*

20 *Since the rabbit is in a sit-down position, mold the bottom part to give it a flat surface for sitting.*

Mold the body into a pear shape by holding the back of the rabbit and pressing it down a few times. Make sure the legs are at a 90° angle with the rabbit's bottom.

21 *Attach the head to the body.*

Balance the head on the body. Use ladder stitch to attach the head. Pay particular attention to tightening the stitches around both sides of the body equally, to avoid having the head lean over to one side.

21-1

21-2

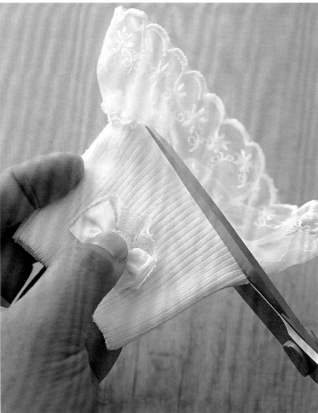

22 *Use a cuff that you have previously cut off to make the hands.*

Cut off the lace part of the cuff for a future necklace. Using the leftover cuff, cut into two parts from the middle.

23 *Turn inside out to stitch each part. Turn them right side out to stuff.*

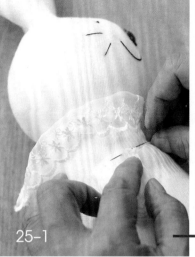

24 *Use a small amount of stuffing to fill the two hands.*

If the hands are too small to fill, use tweezers to push the stuffing into them.

25 *Attach the hands on the side of the body. See the tip below to add a second lace necklace to the rabbit's neck.*

25-1

25-2

Daniel's Classroom Tips

If you want to give the white rabbit some extra color, use the pink sock, and cut off the lace. Put the pink lace on top of the white lace to give the rabbit a more colorful necklace.

India Elephant

STEP BY STEP

Key Tips

1 You need to use socks with curly-edged cuffs. This is the key to making the elephant's flapping ears.

2 Ideally, you want to find patterns on the in-step of the sock. I found the slip-proof sock here with patterns along the instep to give the elephant a henna tattoo.

Materials and Tools

1 Thread, needles, scissors, and marking pen.

2 A pair of children's socks.

3 Two black beads for the eyes. Or you can also use suitable buttons.

4 A decorative button.

5 Stuffing.

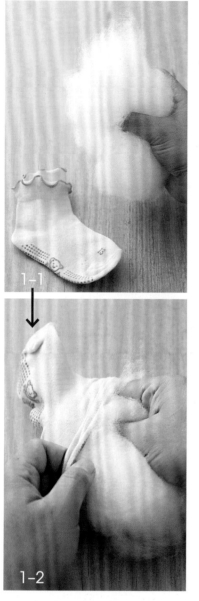

1 *Make the elephant's trunk.*

Get a small ball of stuffing; fill in the toe part of the sock and half of the instep. Make sure you put all stuffing needed in at the same time.

2 *Pull the instep part slightly to extend the length.*

Mold the toe and partial instep of the sock into a long and thin trunk shape. Rub the sides back and forth to give it a uniform shape.

3 *Make the head.*

You will need a larger amount of stuffing. I use a trunk/head ratio of one-to-five. You want around five times the amount of stuffing for the head as you do for the trunk. Push the full amount of stuffing in at once behind the trunk stuffing.

117

4 *Push the stuffing tightly toward the toe.*

Make sure the stuffing is condensed in its position. Tighten the border where the trunk meets the head to give it a clearer outline.

5 *Cut the remaining part of the cuff. Keep the cuff to use as the elephant's ears.*

6 *Seal off the hole where you made the cut.*

How to Make the Body

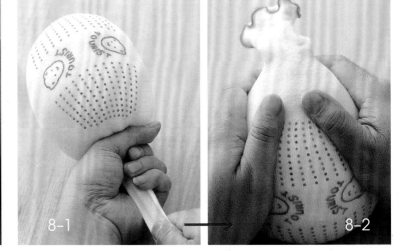

7 *Use the second sock, and measure stuffing slightly more than the amount you used for the head. Push all of the stuffing into the toe and instep of the sock.*

8 *Mold the body.*

Push the stuffing toward the toe, and make sure the body stuffing is condensed into a ball shape. Compare the size of the head to the size of the body, and make sure they are in the right proportion. Mold the body into a pear shape.

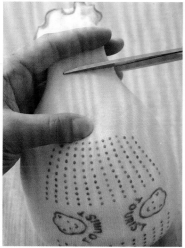
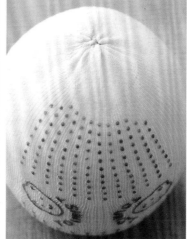

9 Cut the remaining cuff off. It will be used as the elephant's ears.

10 Seal off the hole where you made the cut.

11 Take the cuffs that you cut off from both socks. Cut them into the same size. The curly part of the cuffs will become the elephant's ears.

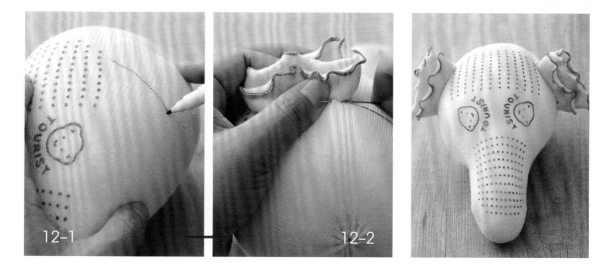

12-1

12-2

12 Draw the positions of the ears on each side of the elephant's head. Stitch the curly cuffs onto the head.

13 Now you have a finished elephant head with two flapping ears.

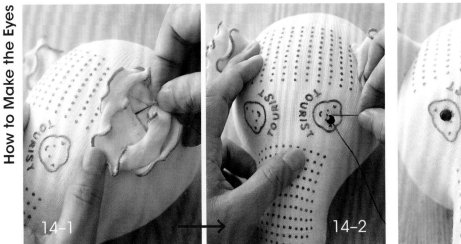

14-1 → 14-2

14 *I used the pattern on the instep as the outline of the eyes. If you can't find socks with patterns that highlight the eyes, sew on two larger buttons as the eyes.*

Let the needle first go through the ear to hide the entry knot. Sew two black beads tightly onto the sock material. You don't want to have floppy eyes hanging off.

15 *Make sure the eyes are positioned evenly on either side of the trunk.*

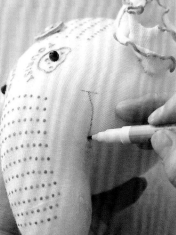

16 *Sew the button in the middle of the forehead. Let the needle go through some of the stuffing with the thread pulled tautly.*

Pick a colorful button that has some flair.

17 *Press the trunk downward.*

Stitch where the underside of the trunk touches the body. Use the ladder stitch to go through part of the stuffing and make the trunk lean toward the body.

18 *Draw a smiley face under the trunk.*

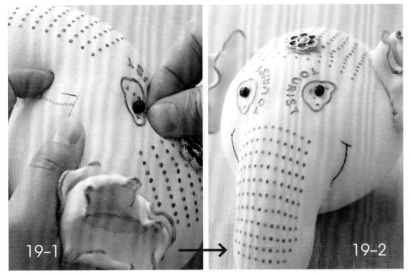

19-1 → 19-2

19 *Use the slip stitch to outline the smiling mouth. You can hide the entry knot underneath the eye.*

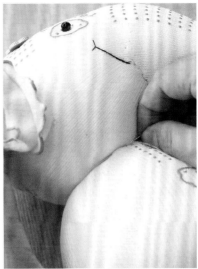

20 *Join the elephant's head and body together in the right position. Stitch the two parts together.*

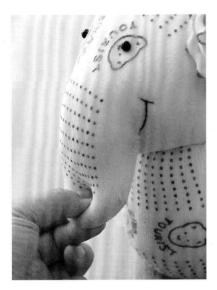

21 *Press the end of the trunk down and shape it so that it curls toward the body.*

Daniel's Classroom Tips

The vivid look on the elephant's face is very much dependent on the type of socks you pick. If you don't want to make an Indian elephant, you can create an elephant with your own flavor. Your creation's unique look is as limitless as your imagination.

Because the elephant has a long trunk, it might tend to lean forward. If so, you can use some of the leftover socks and roll the material into a circle. Try to sit the elephant into the circle cushion to give it a sturdier, flatter bottom. We used this technique in the Lucky Cat project (see page 96).

Teddy Bear

Key Tips

1 I prefer to use a single-colored sock for this doll, though it might not be easy for you to get a bright yellow sock like the one I have used here.

2 The pointed three-dimensional nose is the critical part when sewing the bear.

3 Note the technique on the stuffing, which makes the teddy appear to be half laying down.

Materials and Tools

1 Thread, needle, pins, scissors, marking pen, and tweezers.

2 A pair of yellow children's socks.

3 Two small black beads.

4 A round-shaped button (to be used as the nose tip).

5 Stuffing.

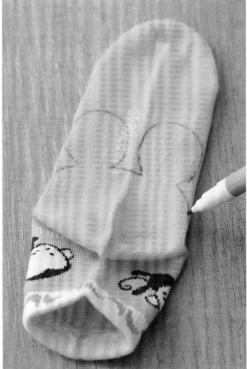

1 *Fold the sock as shown.*

Around half way between the toe and heal, draw the shape of the Teddy's ears and head.

2 *Cut along the marking to use the bottom part as the head.*

Make sure you keep the remaining top part to use as the bear's hands and nose.

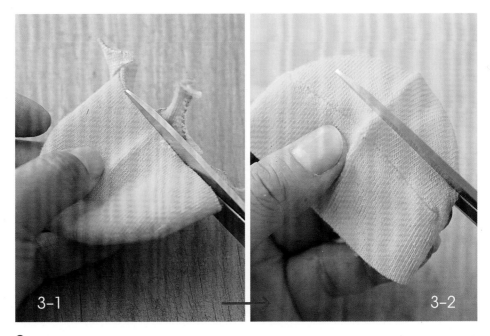

3-1

3-2

3 *Cut off the uneven edges of the toe part.*

Just above the toe line, cut off the toe part to use as the round nose. You will use the remaining part for the hands.

4 To make the hands, fold the hand part of the material in half. Cut off and round one of the edges.

5 Turn the sock inside out, and use backstitch to sew the ears and hands.

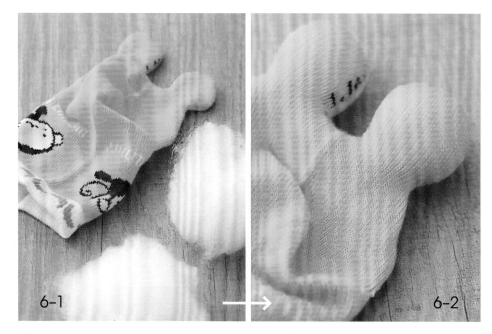

6-1

→

6-2

6 Take two small balls of stuffing and stuff them into each ear.

Make sure you mold the stuffing into a smooth ball shape.

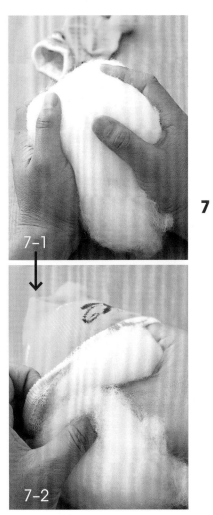

7 *Take a larger amount of stuffing, mold it into a ball shape, and stuff into the head area all at once.*

7-1

7-2

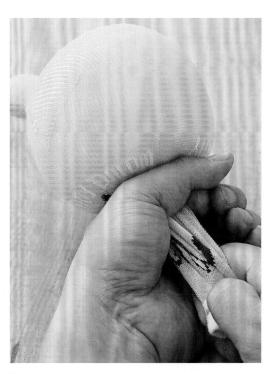

8 *Pull the sock tightly around the bottom of the head.*

Squeeze all stuffing tightly into the head area to ensure a densely filled, round head.

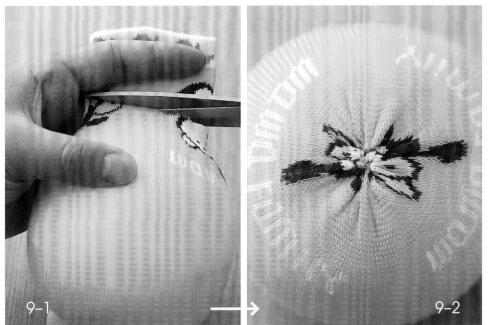

9-1

9-2

9 *Cut off the extra sock at the bottom.*

Seal off the hole at the bottom of the head. You can keep the cuff part you just cut off to use for decorations.

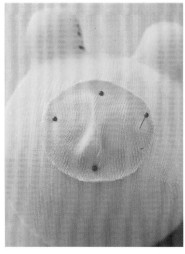

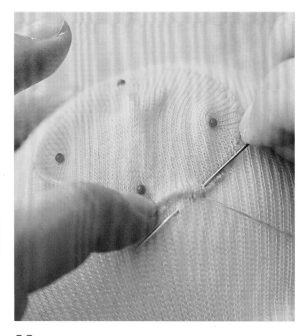

10 *Now we are ready to sew on the nose.*

Use the toe part you cut off from Step 3 as the nose material. It should be a round shape when you open it up and pin it to the proper location on the head.

11 *Use the ladder stitch to sew the nose on the head.*

While you sew, you want to try to hide the seam beneath the material as much as possible. I push the edge in slightly, about 1⁄16 inch (0.1 cm), with each stitch.

12-1 → 12-2

12 *Leave a small gap on the bottom.*

Use tweezers to fill in the nose area, as densely as possible. Make a round, pointed nose. Once you're finished stuffing, continue to stitch the nose opening to the head.

13 *Sew the round button on the tip of the nose.*

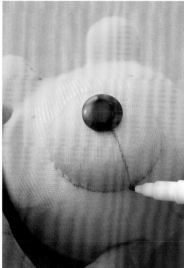

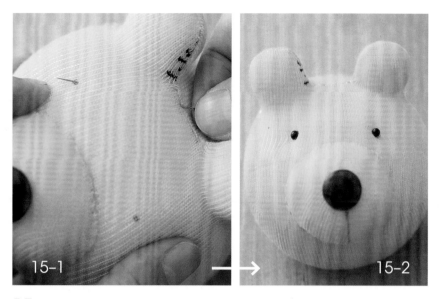

14 *Draw the mouth and eyes on the face.*

15 *Sew on the two small black beads as the eyes of the bear.*

You can start the needle from the seam on the top of the head to hide the knot there.

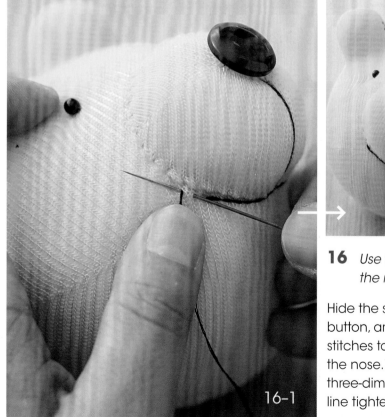

16 *Use the split stitch to outline the nose and the mouth.*

Hide the starting knot under the button, and make the mouth stitches taut along the bottom of the nose. The nose will look more three-dimensional with the mouth line tightened.

17 *Use the other sock, and cut it down the middle, from the toe, along the sock fold line, about 2 inches (5 cm) in length.*

Make sure you curve the edges, to give the feet a cute, round look.

18 *Use backstitch to seal the edges of the feet. Turn the sock inside out first to hide the stitches.*

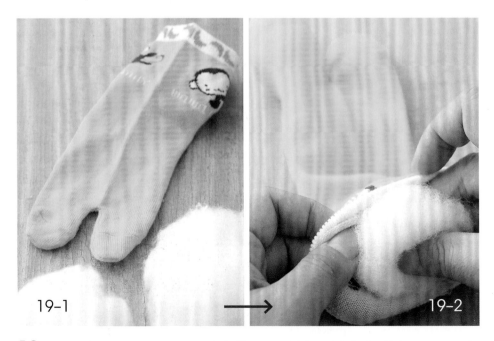

19–1

19–2

19 *Take two small bunches of stuffing, mold them into ball shapes, and fill the feet area.*

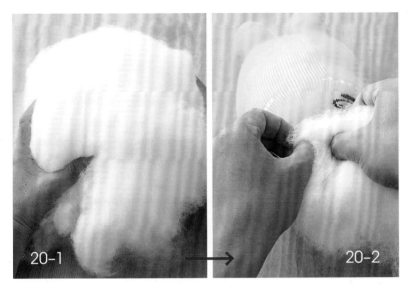

20 *Take a large amount of stuffing and fill the body. You want the head and body to be in the right proportion.*

If the body is too big or too small, resize, and re-mold the stuffing. Finally, mold the stuffing into a pear shape, which will make the bear look like it is half lying down.

21 *Stitch the opening of the body shut.*

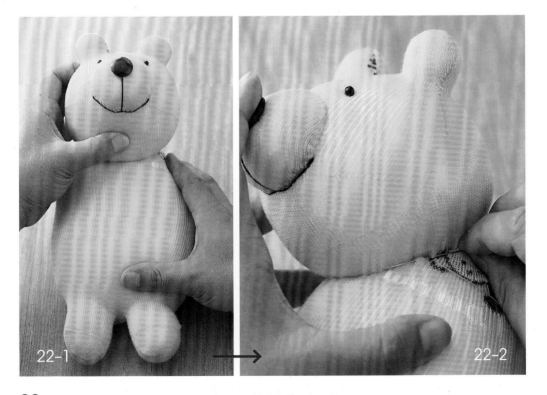

22 *Position the head above the body, in the center.*

The head should be tilted slightly forward, as if the bear is half lying down. Ladder stitch the head and body parts together, starting from the side to hide the knot.

23-1

23-2

23   Take two small balls of stuffing for the hands. Since you've already stitched the hands in Step 5, all you have to do now is stuff the hands with stuffing.

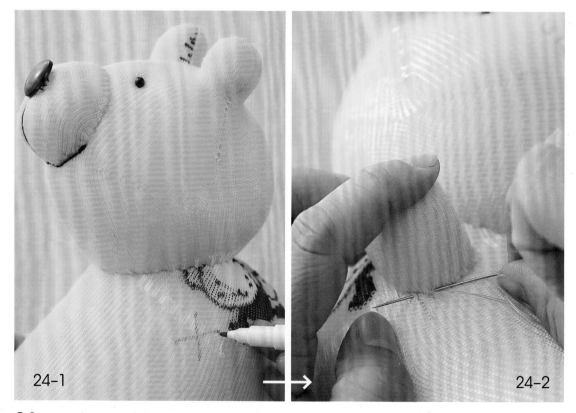

24-1

24-2

24   Mark the location of the hands on each side of the body. Stitch the hands onto the body.

25-1

25-2

25 *You might have some leftover cuffs that you've cut off from Step 9.*

Now you can use the cuff as the bear's necklace.

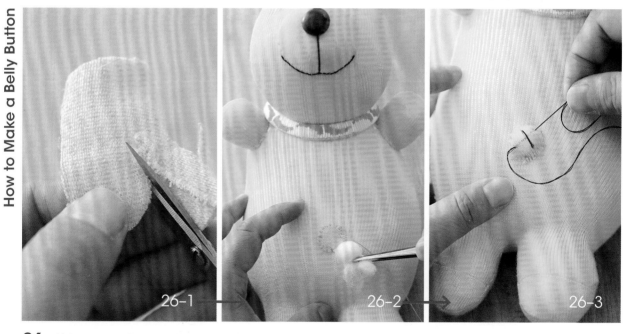

26-1

26-2

26-3

26 *You can cut a small piece of sock from the extra material that you have.*

Sew it onto the bear's stomach, where the belly button is supposed to be. Leave a gap to fill in some stuffing with tweezers, then stitch the gap shut. Finally, sew a cross pattern on top of the belly button with thick, black thread. Now you have a teddy with a cute belly button!

Punk Zebra

STEP BY STEP

Key Tips

1 Molding the stuffing into the desired zebra shape can be tricky with this one. You might need some practice.

2 The buttons for the eyes are one of the key components to giving your zebra a vivid expression. I chose buttons that outline the large, round eyes. You can try this with different buttons, to give the zebra whatever desired expression you'd like.

Materials and Tools

1 Needles, thread, scissors, and marking pen.

2 A pair of striped socks. It will work best if the sock is in black/brown and white stripes, with a solid color block on the heel and toe area. The solid heel area color will be great as the mouth/nose of the zebra.

3 A number of buttons to be used for the eyes, nose, and other decorations if you'd like.

4 A small ball of yarn to be used as the zebra's mane.

5 Stuffing.

1 *The instep part of the sock will become the face.*

2 *Take a small amount of stuffing, and mold it into a ball.*

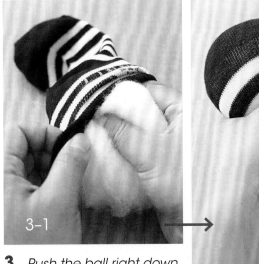

3-1

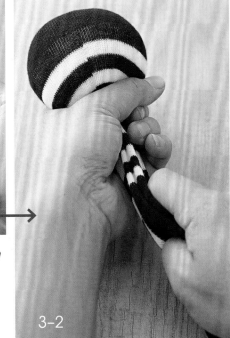

3-2

3 *Push the ball right down to the heel part of the sock.*

Pull the sock tight to push all stuffing into the bottom. Make sure the heel part has a smooth, round finish. This will be the zebra's mouth and nose.

4 *Take another bigger ball of stuffing.*

The amount should be around 1½–2 times the amount of stuffing you used for the mouth. Mold it into an oval shape and fill in behind the mouth.

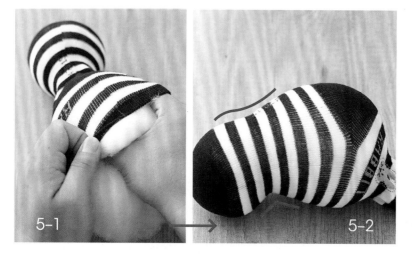

5-1

5-2

5 *Join the two parts of stuffing together.*

At the joint, try to make the upper part of the face a smooth transition. With the bottom part, separate the joint with an angle like **∧**. (See Image 5-2). The face and mouth must have two separate stuffing parts. This project is different from the others, where I previously emphasized putting the stuffing in all at once.

6 *Pull the remaining sock cuff slightly, cut off the extra sock, and keep it for the ears.*

8-1

How to Make the Ears

8-2

7 *Stitch the opening at the bottom of the head shut.*

8 *From Step 6, use the cut off part of the socks to make the ears.*

Fold the piece in the middle and cut through. Round the edges, as show in Image 8-2.

9 *Make sure the ear pieces are inside out, then backstitch to sew the edges together.*

Turn the ears right side out, fold each ear in half, and stitch the bottom parts together tautly. (See Image 9–2.)

10 *Draw the position of the ears on the sides of the head.*

Stitch the ears onto the head. Make sure the ears are symmetrical.

11 *You can press in the middle of the ear shapes to give them hollow parts, which will make them look more like holes.*

12 *I picked round, white buttons to use as the zebra's nostrils. Then I used black thread to sew a cross through the buttons.*

13 *Pick two buttons smaller than the nostril buttons to use as the zebra's eyes.*

Position the eyes two-thirds of the way up from the nostrils. Use black thread to sew a line through the button holes, to form the pupils of the eyes.

14 *You want to shape the mouth and bottom of the face with a distinct angle ∧ shape.*

Use your thumb to press the stuffing down at the joint. Press slightly down on the mouth with your other hand.

15-1

15-2

15 *Now cut the other sock along the fold line, from the toe up, for 2 inches (5 cm). Round the front toe edges.*

16 *Turn the sock inside out, and backstitch all the leg openings together.*

17 *Cut off about 1⅛ inches (3 cm) from the cuff edge. Make sure you have a straight cut. The cut-off cuff will become the zebra's front feet.*

18–1

18–2

18 *Take two small balls of stuffing. Push them into the bottoms of the legs. Stuff them into round-shaped feet.*

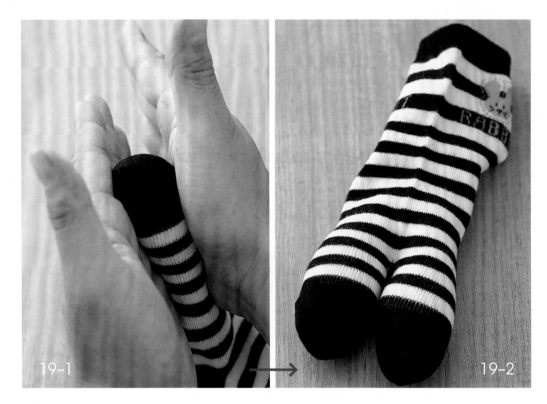

19 *Knead with both hands to make both legs look round and uniform.*

20 *Take a large amount of stuffing, and stuff it into the body of the zebra, right above the two legs you just filled.*

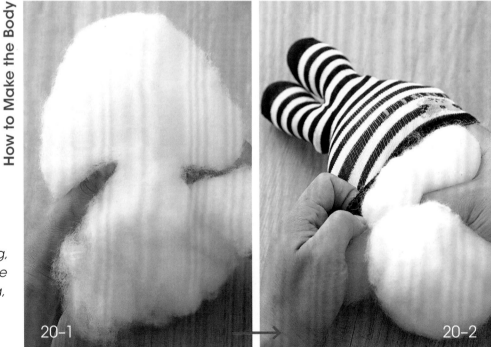

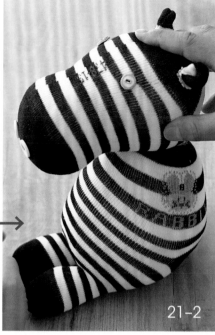

21-1

21-2

21 *Mold the body into a pear shape with a flat bottom, so that the zebra can sit.*

Compare the size of the head and the body while you mold the body, to make sure the body is proportioned slightly bigger than the head.

22 *Position the head on top of the neck part of the body.*

You want the nose to be at a 90-degree angle to the body.

23 *Stitch the head on top of the body; start from the side.*

Use tight ladder stitches and pull thread taut. Make sure you secure the head tightly on the body. If you stitch too loosely, the head might look like it's about to fall off.

How to Make the Front Legs

24 *From Step 17, you have kept two small pieces of cuffs. Turn them inside out first, and stitch the edges.*

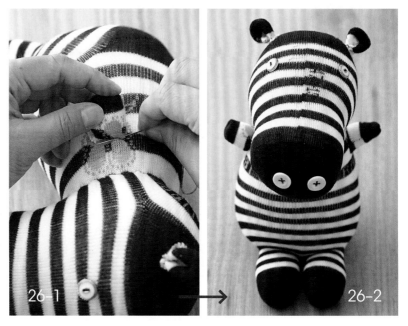

26-1

26-2

25 *Stuff the two front legs with a small amount of stuffing.*

26 *Mark the location of the front legs on the body and sew them in place.*

Make sure both legs are placed symmetrically on the sides of the body.

27 *Decorate the zebra with buttons.*

I used three wooden buttons on its chest.

How to Make the Mane

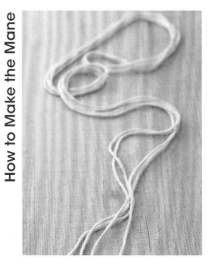

28 *Take a piece of yarn that is at least two feet long.*

Fold the yarn from end to end twice, to make a four-ply string.

140

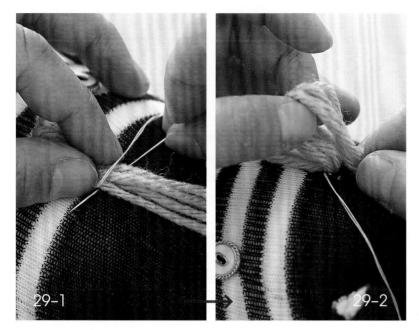

29 *Attach the yarn to the zebra's body.*

Put one end of the yarn bundle on the zebra's forehead, just above the eyes. Backstitch the end of the yarn bundle onto the head. Pull the thread tautly to secure the yarn on the head. Hold the yarn up to form a loop, and stitch the bottom of the loop onto the head. Repeat the steps to form the fluffy mane.

30 *Stitch the yarn along the head until you reach the neck line.*

31 *Cut through each loop, and trim the ends. Now you have a punk zebra.*

Bead-Eyed Hippo

STEP BY STEP

Key Tips

1 I like to make a funny looking hippo with very small eyes, just to contrast the huge head.

2 Push the stuffing into the head part all at once to give it an overall smooth look.

3 The final shape of the hippo is critical for giving it a cute look.

Materials and Tools

1 Thread, needles, scissors, and marking pen.

2 Two pure-white socks, plus a pair of colorful socks. (You can use children's or adult's socks, depending on what size hippo you prefer.)

3 Two black mini beads.

4 A large, round black button.

5 Stuffing.

1 *Depending on how big you want your hippo to be, you can adjust the size of the stuffing.*

2 *Push all of the stuffing toward the toe part of the sock; densely fill the toe and instep.*

3 *Add another ball of stuffing.*

The second ball of stuffing should be smaller than the first amount of stuffing you used in Step 1. (See Image 4-1)

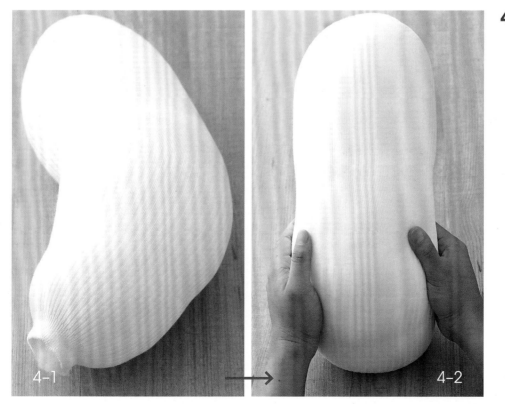

4-1

4-2

4 *Once the sock is filled with two balls of stuffing, mold it into a column, with a smooth, round shape on the top.*

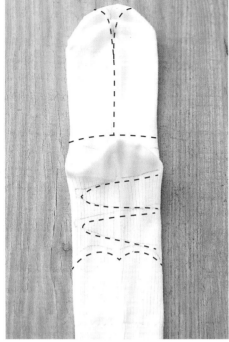

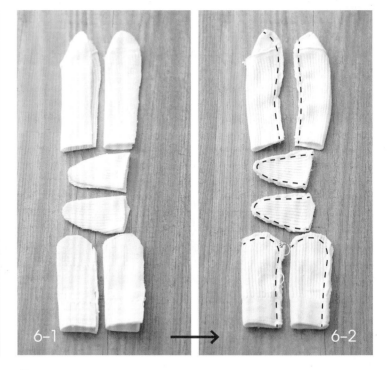

5 *Take another sock, and mark the shape of the feet, ears, and front legs as illustrated in the photo.*

Use the toe and instep of the sock for the feet. The tube part of the sock will become the ears and front legs.

6 *Cut off the different parts along the marking. Turn them inside out and stitch the edges together.*

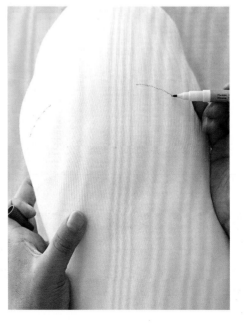

7 *Stuff the ears.*

Mold the stuffing with pointed tip at the end.

8 *Mark the position of the ears, slightly toward the back of the head.*

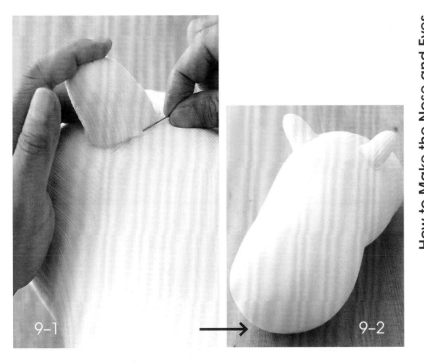

9 *Stitch the ears onto the head using the ladder stitch.*

10 *Sew the black button in the middle of the front nose area as the hippo's nose.*

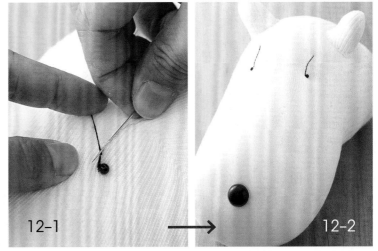

12 *Sew the beads at the marked location.*

Pull the thread tautly so the bead creates a dimple in the stuffing. Sew the thin line above the eyes for the eyebrows.

11 *Draw the position of the two small eyes and long, thin eyebrows.*

13 *Cut off the leftover sock at the end of the head.*

Seal off the opening with straight stitches. Make sure you close off the opening with dense stitches, since you have a large amount of stuffing inside.

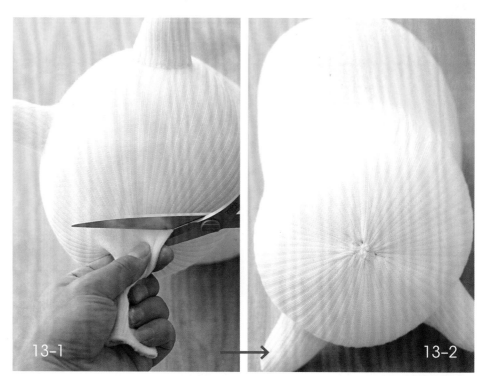

13-1

13-2

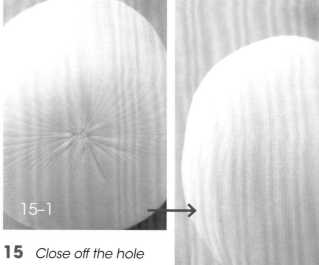

15-1

15-2

14 *Using the same technique as in Steps 1 and 2, fill another sock with stuffing to form the body. Be sure that the head appears longer and slightly bigger than the body. Cut off the extra sock tube.*

15 *Close off the hole at the bottom of the body.*

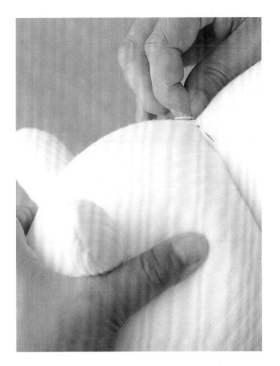

16 *Position the head on top of the body, and stitch them together with dense ladder stitches.*

17 *Use the tubes that you already stitched from Step 6.*

Stuff them with stuffing. Condense the stuffing into the tubes to make them firm. For the smaller front legs, leave a small section on the end empty.

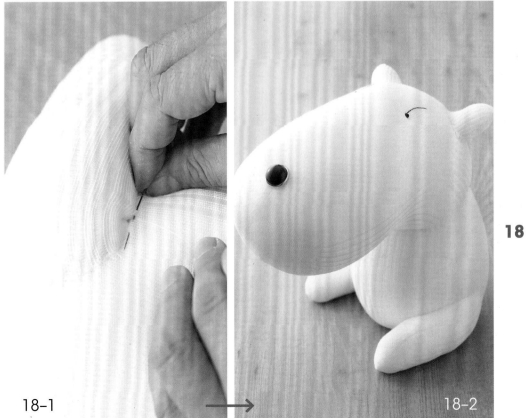

18-1

18-2

18 *Stitch the feet onto the body. Attach part of the feet to the side of the body to curve the legs slightly around the body.*

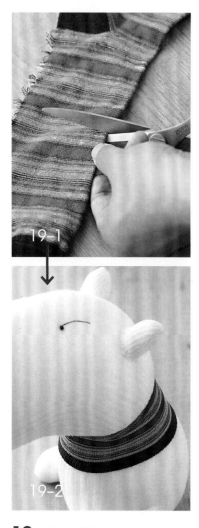

19 Cut off the tube and cuff part of the colorful sock, and put it over the hippo's neck as his necklace.

20 Sew the front legs on the side of the body, right below the head.

How to Make the Tail

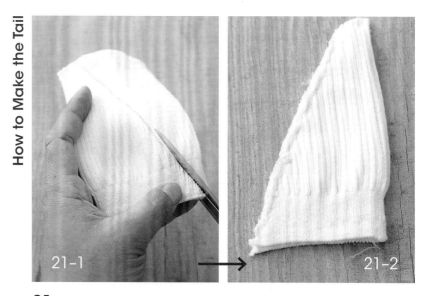

21 Use the leftover sock material, and cut it into a triangle shape. Sew the edges together.

22-1

22-2

22 *Stuff the tail and stitch it the back of the body. The tail will stabilize the head-heavy hippo and allow it to sit straight.*

23 *You've finished the hippo—large head with tiny eyes, just the sort of hippo I like!*

Daniel's Classroom Tips

If you are making larger sock dolls, you want to be sure to use plenty of stuffing and close stitches. You want the sock to be filled tightly to give it the fullness of the shape.

You might want to practice mini sock dolls first before attempting to make larger dolls. It is a lot easier to get the correct proportion on smaller dolls than on larger ones.

When sewing the larger dolls, you want to use strong thread with tight stitches.

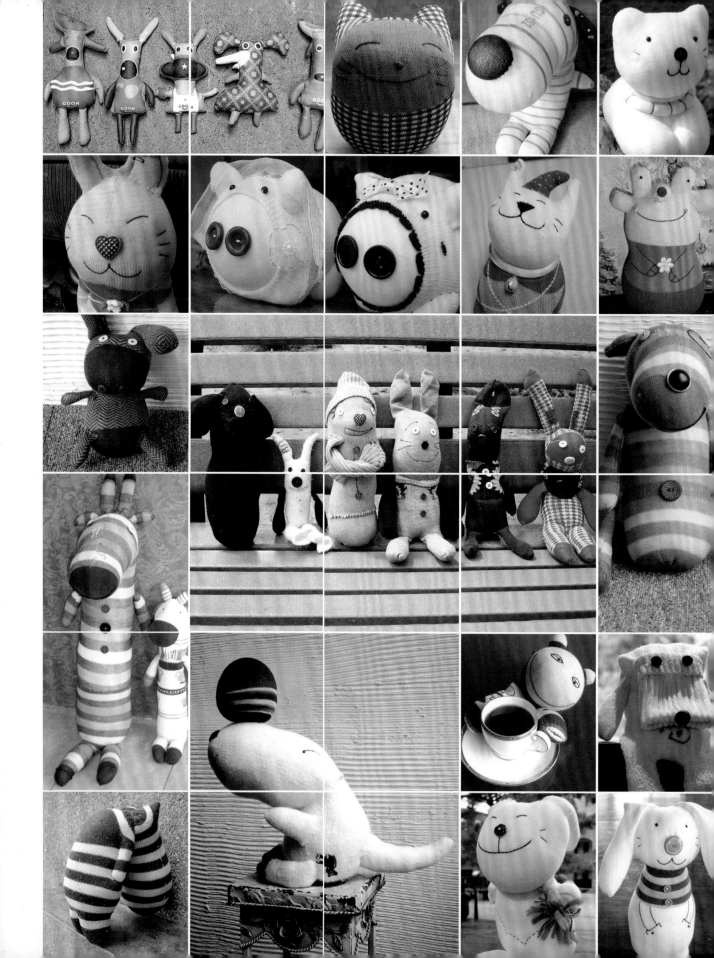

Gallery of Sock Dolls